MARGARET MORGAN
and
MARY MORGAN PEDLOW

Memorial

RIVERSIDE PUBLIC LIBRARY

Egg Carton MANIA

Christine M. Irvin

Children's Press®

A Division of Scholastic Inc.

New York • Toronto • London • Auckland • Sydney

Mexico City • New Delhi • Hong Kong

Danbury, Connecticut

The author and publisher are not responsible for injuries or accidents that occur during or from any craft projects. Craft projects should be conducted in the presence of or with the help of an adult. Any instructions of the craft projects that require the use of sharp or other unsafe items should be conducted by or with the help of an adult.

Design and Production by Function Thru Form Inc.
Illustrations by Mia Gomez, Function Thru Form Inc.
Photographs ©: School Tools/Joe Atlas

Library of Congress Cataloging-in-Publication Data

Irvin, Christine M.
　　Egg carton mania / by Christine M. Irvin
　　　　p. cm. — (Craft mania)
　　Includes index.
　　ISBN 0-516-22277-5 (lib. bdg.)　　　　　　　　0-516-27758-8 (pbk.)
　　1. Egg carton craft—Juvenile literature. [1. Egg carton craft. 2. Handicraft.] I. Title. II. Series.

　　TT870 .I7424 2001
　　745.5—dc21

　　　　　　　　　　　　　　　　　　　　　　　　　00-065647

CHILDREN'S PRESS and associated logos are trademarks and or registered trademarks of Grolier Publishing Co., Inc.
SCHOLASTIC and associated logos are trademarks and or registered trademarks of Scholastic Inc.

1 2 3 4 5 6 7 8 9 10 R 11 10 09 08 07 06 05 04 03 02

CHILDREN'S ROOM

Table of Contents

Welcome to the World of
CRAFT MANIA!

Don't throw away that egg carton! Everyday items, such as egg cartons, cardboard tubes, and paper plates, can become exciting works of art. You can have fun doing the projects and help save the environment at the same time by recycling these household objects instead of just throwing them away.

You can find ways to reuse many things around your home in craft projects. Bottle caps, buttons, old dried beans, and seeds can become eyes, ears, or a nose for an animal. Instead of buying construction paper, you can use scraps of wrapping paper or even last Sunday's comics to cover your art projects. Save the twist ties from bags of bread or vegetables—they make great legs! These are just a few examples of how you can turn garbage into art. Try to think of other things in your home that can be used in your crafts.

♻ Did You Know?

- Each person creates about 4 pounds (1.8 kilograms) of garbage per day.

- Each person in the United States uses about 580 pounds (260 kg) of paper every year. Businesses in the United States use enough paper to circle the earth 20 times every day!

- Americans use enough cardboard each year to make a paper bale as big as a football field.

- Americans throw away more than 60 billion food and drink cans (like tin cans and soft drink cans) and 28 billion glass bottles and jars (like those from ketchup and pickles) every year.

That's a lot of trash!

What you will need

It's easy to get started on your craft projects. The crafts in this book require some materials you can find around your home, some basic art supplies, and your imagination.

Buttons, bottle caps, beads, old dried beans or seeds for decoration

Glue

Tape

Tempera paints

Colored markers

Hole puncher

Construction paper (or newspaper or scraps of wrapping paper)

Felt (or scraps of fabric)

Twist ties (or pipe cleaners)

Safety scissors

You might want to keep your craft materials in a box so that they will be ready any time you want to start a craft project. Now that you know what you need, look through the book and pick a project to try. Become a Craft Maniac!

A Note to Grown-Ups

Older children will be able to do most of the projects by themselves. Younger ones will need more adult supervision. All of them will enjoy making the items and playing with their finished creations. The directions for most of the crafts in this book require the use of scissors. Do not allow young children to use scissors without adult supervision.

☞ Helpful Hints

Some egg cartons are made of paper, and some are made of polystyrene. Either kind will work for the projects in this book. If you use polystyrene cartons, you do not want to paint them. Tempera paint chips off easily from this type of carton. Another tip for polystyrene cartons is to use tacky glue instead of white glue. Use a ballpoint pen to poke holes in egg cartons. Ask your friends and relatives to save their egg cartons for you.

Army of Ants

What you need

- **One egg carton**
  (will make four ants)
- **Scissors** (Before cutting any material, please ask an adult for help.)
- **Tempera paints**
- **Paintbrush**
- **Pen**
- **Seven twist ties**
  (for legs and antennae)
- **Glue**

What you do

1 Cut the egg carton. Have an adult help you cut a three-cup section from the egg carton, as shown. Then, paint the egg carton section with the tempera paint. Let the paint dry before going on to Step 2.

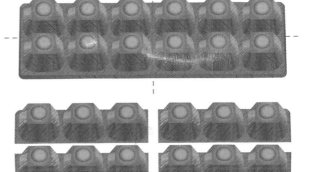

2 Make some legs. Using a pen, have an adult help you punch three small holes in each side of the ant's body. Thread one twist tie in through a hole on one side of the body. Wrap the twist tie around itself to form one of the legs, as shown. Repeat this for the remaining five holes. Bend the ends of the twist ties to form feet.

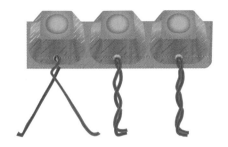

3 Add the antennae. Glue a twist tie to the top of one of the egg sections.

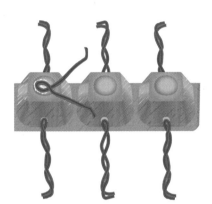

4 Add the face. Use paint, markers, or crayons to create the face for your ant.

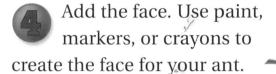
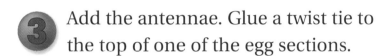

Other Ideas

- Make an army of ants. Use the rest of the egg carton to make three more ants, for a total of four ants. Make as many ants as you want for your army.

- Paint your ants different colors, such as red for army ants and brown for carpenter ants.

Collection Box

What you need

- One egg carton for each collection box
- Tempera paints
- Paintbrush
- Seeds, beads, or glitter
- Glue
- Hole puncher
- Two 6-inch-long pieces of ribbon
- One piece of scrap cardboard

What you do

1 Paint the egg carton. Using tempera paints, paint the outside of the egg carton any colors you like. Let the paint dry before going on to Step 2.

2 Decorate the egg carton. Use a scrap of cardboard to spread a thin layer of glue on the top of the egg carton. Sprinkle seeds, beads, or glitter lightly onto the glue. Let the glue dry. Then, hold the box upside down over a trash can and gently tap off the excess seeds, beads, or glitter.

3 Add a fastener to your collection box. Using the hole puncher, make two holes in egg carton, one on the top front edge and one on the bottom front edge, as shown. Thread the end of one of the ribbons in through the hole of the top part of the carton. Tie the ribbon around the hole in the carton, as shown. Do the same thing with the other ribbon on the bottom part of the egg carton. Tie the loose ends of the ribbons together to close your collection box.

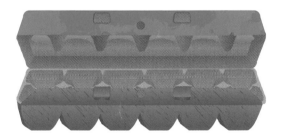

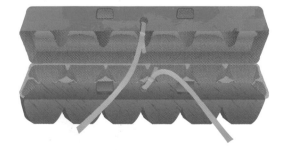

Other Ideas

- Paint the outside of your collection box one color and the inside another color.

- Use your collection box as a jewelry box, or store your special collection of rocks or other small items in your box.

- Make a collection box for a special friend. Paint the box your friend's favorite color or colors. Give the collection box to your friend as a birthday gift or just as a special present for a special friend.

Spooky Spider

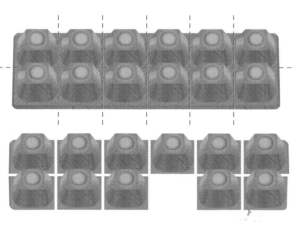

What you need

- **One egg carton** (will make twelve spiders)
- **Scissors** (Before cutting any material, please ask an adult for help.)
- **Tempera paints**
- **Paintbrush**
- **Pen**
- **Eight twist ties** (for legs)
- **Markers**

What you do

1. Make the spider's body. Have an adult help you cut a one-cup section from the egg carton, as shown. Then, paint the spider's body with tempera paint. Let the paint dry before going on to Step 2.

12

2 Give your spider some legs. Using a pen, have an adult help you poke eight small holes in the one-cup section. Thread a twist tie through one of the holes. Wrap the ends of the twist tie together to form the leg, as shown. Repeat this process with the seven remaining twist ties to add the rest of the legs.

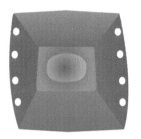

3 Add a face. Use markers, crayons, or paints to add the face for your spider.

Other Ideas

- Cover your spider with bits of furry fabric to make a really hairy, scary spider.

- Make a spider mobile using several spiders. You can paint them all the same color or paint them different colors. Have an adult help you poke a small hole in the top of each spider. Thread different lengths of yarn or string up through the holes in each spider and tie a knot in the end of the yarn underneath each spider to hold the yarn in place. Hang your spiders from a coat hanger or from the ceiling to make your mobile.

Flower Power

What you need

- **One egg carton**
  (will make twelve flowers)

- **Scissors** (Before cutting any
  material, please ask an adult
  for help.)

- **Tempera paints**

- **Paintbrush**

- **Pen**

- **One twig for stem**

- **Glue**

- **Green construction paper
  for leaves**

What you do

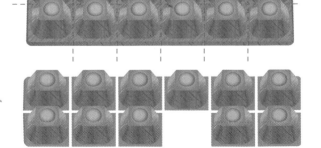

1 Make the flower's head. Have an adult help you cut out a one-cup section of the egg carton, as shown. Then, paint the flower with tempera paints, using any colors you like. Let the paint dry before going on to Step 2.

2 Add a stem. Using the pen, have an adult help you poke a small hole through the bottom of your flower, as shown. Place glue around the hole. Put one end of the twig through the hole. Let the glue dry before going on to Step 3.

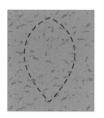

3 Add the leaves. Cut the construction paper into leaf shapes, as shown. Glue the leaves on the twig.

Other Ideas

- Add petals to your flower. Cut petals out of construction paper and glue them on the egg carton section.

- Use a pipe cleaner for a stem instead of a twig.

- Create a flower magnet. Make only the top of the flower using one egg-cup section. Glue a magnet to the back and stick it on the refrigerator.

Double-Decker Bus

What you need

- Two egg cartons
- Glue
- Scissors (Before cutting any material, please ask an adult for help.)

- Six large buttons or bottle caps, all the same size, for wheels
- Markers
- Crayons

What you do

1 Glue one egg carton shut. Spread a layer of glue around the edge of one egg carton. Press the lid down to hold it in place.

2 Have an adult help you cut the top off the other egg carton. Save the lid for the top of the double-decker bus.

16

3 Add the lid to the other egg carton. Spread glue on the top of the lid of the egg carton. Press the egg carton lid in place on top of the other egg carton, as shown. Let the glue dry before going on to Step 4.

place along the bottom edge of the bus. Spread glue on the other buttons and glue them in place, as shown. Let the glue dry. Once the glue is dry, turn the egg carton structure over and glue the buttons on to the other side. Let the glue dry before going on to Step 5.

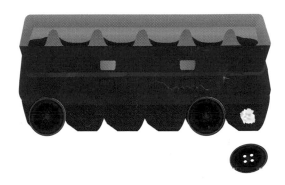

4 Add the wheels. Place the egg carton structure on one side. Spread glue on the flat side of one of the buttons. Press the button in

5 Decorate your bus. Draw in windows and doors with markers or crayons.

Other Ideas

- Paint your bus with tempera paints.
- Make a delivery truck by skipping Steps 2 and 3. You do not need to add a top deck. Just glue on buttons for wheels and draw in windows and doors.

Finger Puppets

What you need

- **One egg carton** (will make six puppets)
- **Scissors** (Before cutting any material, please ask an adult for help.)
- **Tempera paint**
- **Paintbrush**
- **Markers**

What you do

1 Cut out the puppet's body. Have an adult help you cut a two-cup section from the egg carton, as shown. Fold the section in half, so one cup opens above the other cup, as shown.

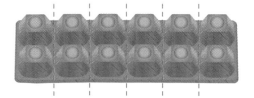

2 Make the finger holes. Have an adult help you cut two holes in the back of the puppet big enough for your fingers to fit through, as shown.

3 Paint your puppet with tempera paint. Use any color you like. Let the paint dry before going on to Step 4.

4 Give your puppet a face. Using the markers, draw eyes, eyelashes, lips, and a nose.

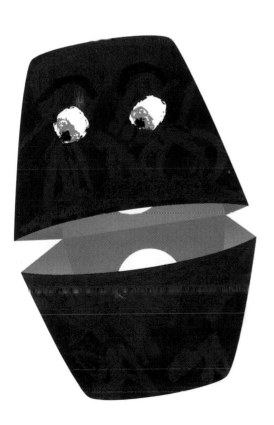

Other Ideas

- Add scraps of yarn to the tops of your finger puppets for hair.

- Make several puppets and paint each of them a different color.

- Make a family of finger puppets.

- Make finger puppets to match your favorite characters in a book, like *Goldilocks and the Three Bears.* You would need Papa Bear, Mama Bear, Baby Bear, and Goldilocks.

Lucky Ladybug

What you need

- **One egg carton**
  (will make twelve ladybugs)
- **Scissors** (Before cutting any
  material, please ask an adult for help.)
- **Red tempera paint**
- **Paintbrush**
- **Markers**
- **Tape**
- **Three small black pipe
  cleaners** (for the legs)
- **Black construction paper**
  (to cover the bottom of the ladybug)
- **Glue**

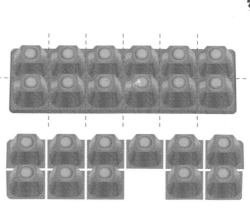

What you do

1. Make the ladybug's body. Have an adult help you cut a one-cup section from the egg carton, as shown. Then, paint your ladybug with the red tempera paint. Let the paint dry before going on to Step 2.

2 Add the ladybug's spots. Using a black marker, draw a line down the middle of the ladybug's body. Then, draw black spots on both sides of the black line, as shown.

3 Add the eyes. Using the black marker, draw two small dots on the ladybug's face.

4 Place the ladybug on the black construction paper. Using a red marker, trace around the outside of the ladybug's body, as shown. Have an adult help you cut out the shape.

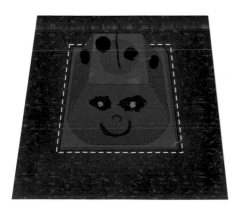

5 Add the legs. Place the pipe cleaners on the construction paper, making sure the legs hang out the same amount on both sides of the paper. Tape the legs in place on the paper.

6 Finish your ladybug. Spread a thin layer of glue around the bottom edge of the ladybug's body. Place the paper piece, with the legs, on the bottom of the ladybug, with the legs glued to the bottom of the ladybug's body. Make sure the pipe cleaner legs stick out the sides of your ladybug. Let the glue dry before playing with your ladybug.

Other Ideas

- Make different kinds of bugs. Paint your bug brown to look like a stink bug or paint it green to look like a beetle. Use your imagination and make your own bugs.

- Glue a ribbon to the bottom of your ladybug and wear it as a bracelet.

Mancala

What you need

- One polystyrene egg carton
- **Scissors** (Before cutting any material, please ask an adult for help.)
- **Glue**
- **Forty-eight small stones, buttons, or dried beans**

What you do

1 Have an adult help you cut the lid off the egg carton. Now cut the lid in half, as shown. The two halves will be used for the Mancala cups.

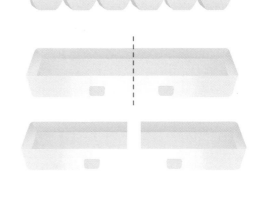

2 Add the Mancala cups. Turn the bottom of the egg carton upside-down. Spread a layer of glue on the bottoms of two egg-cup sections on one end of the egg carton, as shown. Turn one half of the cut lid upside-down and press in place, as shown. Do the same thing with the other lid section on the other end of the egg carton. Let the glue dry.

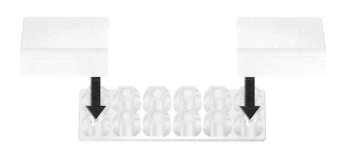

3 Turn the Mancala board right-side up. Use the 48 stones, buttons, or dried beans for your Mancala stones. Play the game according to regular game rules.

Other Ideas

- Paint your Mancala board with tempera paints.

- Use small beads for the Mancala stones.

- If you use stones or dried beans for your Mancala stones, paint them with tempera paints. Use several different colors of paint.

Super Sailboat

What you need

- One polystyrene egg carton
- Scissors
  (Before cutting any material, please ask an adult for help.)
- Pencil
- Paper shopping bag or construction paper
- Glue
- Plastic straw
- Piece of modeling clay
- Ruler

What you do

1 Have an adult help you cut the lid off the egg carton. Use the bottom part of the carton for the base of your boat.

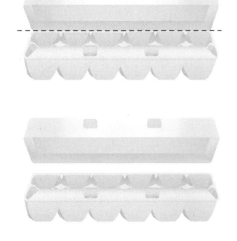

24

2 Make a sail. Using the pencil, draw a triangle on the construction paper. The triangle needs to be about 6 inches by 8 inches by 10 inches, as shown. Have an adult help you cut out the triangle shape. Spread a thin layer of glue along the edge of the paper. Place the straw on the glue. Let the glue dry before going on to Step 3.

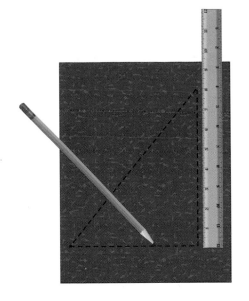

3 Finish your boat. Place a small ball of modeling clay in the center of the egg carton. Push the sail's straw mast down through the clay, as shown. Make sure you have enough clay to hold the straw in place.

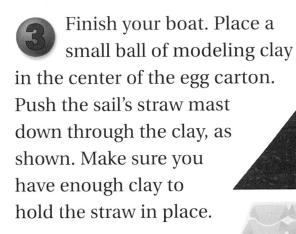

Other Ideas

- Decorate the boat's sail. Color it with markers or paint it before you glue the sail to the straw mast in Step 2.

- Use wallpaper or stiff wrapping paper for the sail.

Playful Pig

What you need

- **One egg carton** (will make 3 pigs)
- **Scissors** (Before cutting any material, please ask an adult for help.)
- **Two small paper plates**
- **Glue**
- **Two small buttons or bottle caps** (for eyes)
- **Construction paper** (for ears)
- **One toothpaste tube cap or large bottle cap** (for the snout)
- **One twist tie** (for the tail)
- **Markers**
- **Pen**

What you do

1 Cut the egg carton. Have an adult help you cut a four-cup section from the egg carton, as shown.

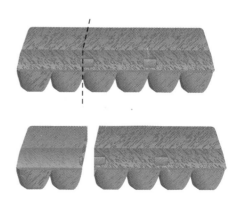

26

2 Make the pig's body. Spread a layer of glue on the inside edge of the four-cup section. Press the lid down to glue it shut. Spread a layer of glue on the top of the lid. Turn one of the paper plates upside down. Press it in place on top of the lid, as shown. Let the glue dry.

3 Add the pig's head. Using the scissors, have an adult help you trim the edge of the paper plate so that it is even with the cut edge of the egg carton, as shown. Spread a layer of glue around the cut section of the egg carton. Turn the other paper plate upside down. Press it in place on the glue, as shown. Let the glue dry.

4 Add the eyes. Spread a layer of glue on the flat sides of the buttons. Press the buttons in place on the pig's head.

5 Add the snout. Spread a layer of glue around the bottom edge of the toothpaste tube cap. Press the cap in place on the pig's head.

6 Add the ears. Have an adult help you cut two ear shapes out of the construction paper, as shown. Spread a layer of glue on one side of each ear shape. Press the ears in place on the pig's head, as shown. Let the glue dry.

7 Add the tail. Using a pen, have an adult help you poke a small hole in the end of top paper plate, as shown. Thread one end of the twist tie through the hole. Twist the end of the twist tie to hold it in place.

Other Ideas

- Make a lion instead of a pig.

Silly Snowman

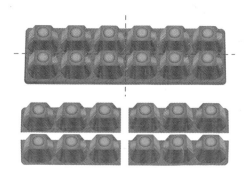

What you need

- **One egg carton**
  (will make two snowmen)

- **Scissors** (Before cutting any material, please ask an adult for help.)

- **Tempera paint**

- **Paintbrush**

- **Glue**

- **Construction paper** (for boots)

- **Markers**

- **Small piece of fabric or long twist tie** (for a scarf)

What you do

1 Cut the egg carton. Have an adult help you cut two three-cup sections from the egg carton, as shown.

2 Glue the two egg carton sections together. Spread a thin layer of glue around the edges of one of the sections. Press the two sections together, as shown. Let the glue dry before going on to Step 3.

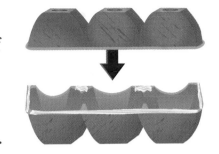

3 Paint your snowman with white tempera paint. Let the paint dry before going on to Step 4.

4 Give your snowman a face. Draw on eyes and a mouth for your snowman using markers.

5 Give your snowman some buttons. Draw button shapes on the snowman's body with markers.

6 Add boots. Have an adult help you cut out two boot shapes from the construction paper, as shown. Glue the boots in place on the bottom of the snowman's body. Let the glue dry before going on to Step 7.

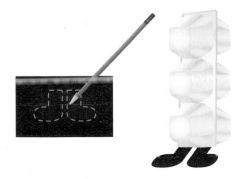

7 Finish your snowman. Wrap a small piece of fabric or the twist tie around the snowman's neck.

Other Ideas

- Use beads or dried beans for the snowman's eyes and buttons, and felt for the nose and mouth.

- Add glitter to make your snowman sparkle.

- Make your snowman into a shaker. Before you glue the two sections together in Step 2, pour some beans or beads or rice (or anything that is dry and will make a noise) in one of the snowman's body sections. Then, press the other section in place and let the glue dry.

Cute Crocodile

- **One egg carton that holds a dozen eggs**
- **One egg carton that holds half a dozen eggs**
- **Paper** (for a tongue)
- **Scissors** (Before cutting any material, please ask an adult for help.)
- **Four bath tissue tubes**
- **Glue**
- **Markers**

What you do

1 Make a tongue. Have an adult help you cut a tongue-shape from the paper. Put a drop of glue on the end of the tongue. Press the tongue in place in the end of the small egg carton, as shown.

2 Glue the small egg carton shut. Spread a layer of glue around

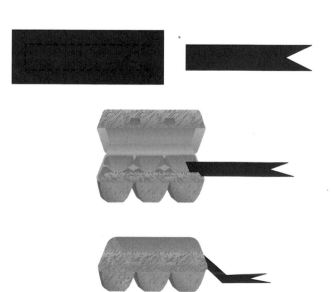

the edges of the small egg carton, as shown. Close the lid and press down.

3 Have an adult help you cut the top off the big egg carton. Save the bottom part of the carton for the crocodile's body.

4 Add some legs. Spread a layer of glue around one end of one of the bath tissue rolls. Press the tissue tube in place in the big egg carton section in the second row from the end. Glue another leg in place right beside it. Glue the other two legs in place on the other end of the carton section, as shown. Let the glue dry before going on to Step 5.

section (the end without the tongue) into the two egg holder cups of the body section, as shown. Let the glue dry before going on to Step 6.

6 Give your crocodile a face. Turn your crocodile over. Draw in eyes and nose holes with markers, as shown.

5 Attach the head to the body. With the crocodile's legs still sticking up in the air, put some glue in the two egg holder cups at one end of the carton section. Press the two egg holder cups of the head

Other Ideas

- Add a tail made from construction paper or newspaper.
- Paint your crocodile with tempera paints.
- Use buttons for the eyes.

Index

About the Author

Christine M. Irvin lives in the Columbus, Ohio area with her husband, her three children, and her dog. She enjoys writing, reading, doing arts and crafts, and shopping.